TAKE BACK YOUR LIFE

103 Highly-Effective Strategies to Snuff Out a Narcissist's Gaslighting and Enjoy the Happy Life You Really Deserve

By Angela Atkinson

A BlissFireMedia Production

Take Back Your Life, Published by

BlissFireMedia, LLC, St. Louis, Missouri

All rights reserved. This book or parts thereof may not be reproduced in any form, stored in any retrieval system, or transmitted in any form by any means - electronic, mechanical, photocopy, recording, or otherwise - without prior written permission of the publisher, except as provided by United States of America copyright law. For permission requests, write to the publisher, at blissfiremedia@gmail.com. For information about special discounts available for bulk purchases, sales promotions, fund-raising and educational needs, contact us at blissfiremedia@gmail.com.

BlissFireMedia.com

QueenBeeing.com

Copyright ©2015 by

Angela Atkinson & BlissFireMedia

Table of Contents

Contents

Gratitude: Please Accept This 'Thank You' Gift.. 7

Dedication 9

Introduction 11

Start on the Road to Emotional Abuse Recovery 15

The 10 Most Important Things You Need to Know if You're in a Toxic Relationship with a Narcissist 17

Mean People Suck: 3 Top Life Hacks for Dealing with Your Everyday, Average Narcissists 21

3 Best Practices for Dealing with Toxic People in Your Life 25

Narcissists in Relationships: Where Gaslighting Begins 31

3 Shocking Common Qualities Among the Partners of Narcissists 35

The 3 Stages of Gaslighting 39

How can you tell if you're being gaslighted? 43

Top 10 Warning Signs You're Being Gaslighted 45

Narcissistic Rage and Narcissistic Injury: 6 Ways to Diffuse a Raging Narcissist 51

Understanding the Hidden Messages in Narcissistic Rage 55

Overcoming Your Narcissist: Top 10 Strategies to Overcome Anger and Gain Peace 59

Top 10 Tips for Enhancing Your Emotional and Mental Health 63

Staying in Control: Crucial Tactics for Managing Panic Attacks 67

    4 Must-Know Facts about Panic Attacks 67

    9 Best Ways to Manage Panic Attacks 68

Self-Confidence Booster: 8 Step Action Plan for Recovering from Narcissistic Manipulation and Abuse 71

6 Tips for Overcoming Adversity 75

8 Ways to Harness the Power of Personal Boundaries 79

Bonus Section: 7 Days to Inner Peace - Daily Affirmations & Reflections for the Victims of Gaslighting and Other Forms of Narcissistic Abuse 83

    Day 1: You Are Blessed. 84

    Day 2: I am the best version of myself 87

    Day 3: I love and approve of myself 90

Day 4: My mind is clear and focused............... 93

Day 5: I deserve the very best in my life........ 96

Day 6: I am growing stronger in body, mind and soul.. 99

Day 7: I am grateful for all of the good things in my life..102

About the Author 105

One Last Thing...109

Other Books by Angie Atkinson............................111

Contact Angie Atkinson................................115

Gratitude: Please Accept This 'Thank You' Gift

I don't claim to have all of the answers to life, but as someone who does her best to make sense of the world, I've learned a few things that have proven invaluable. That's why I became a life coach - I wanted the opportunity to help others to evolve beyond their current potential to become the best possible versions of themselves.

I'm still working on that part, of course, but I've made some pretty significant strides. One of my favorite ways to keep my life on the right track is to continually pay it forward - and that's why I'm going to start this book by first saying THANK YOU to you, my friend and fellow survivor, for buying the book.

Since you were so kind as to support my mission, I'd like to offer you a gift that will help you to change your life even more than this book alone. You can pick it up for free, right here: QueenBeeing.com/freegift.

Dedication

To my children, who inspired my L.O.V.E. Movement. I am so excited and grateful to watch you grow into healthy, happy and fulfilled adults who understand that you are worth loving, and that you deserve to not only define yourself, but to be the master of your own destiny. You get to create your own brand of personal fulfillment. Each of you is amazing and gifted in your own ways: own that and be the best possible version of you. Always remember to set and maintain your own boundaries. Never forget that you are the only YOU in the world, and that I am proud of you for choosing to unconditionally love and accept yourselves. Know that you deserve to be happy, know that you are unique and special and know that you are loved, always and unconditionally.

Introduction

The great automaker and apparent philosopher Henry Ford said, "If you think you can do a thing or think you can't do a thing, you're right."

He was exactly right.

My message to you in this book is simple. The power you seek to change your life is in your hands. All you have to do is use it - and in the case of the verbal abuse you're dealing with (not to mention all of the mental and emotional abuse) at the hands of a narcissist, you're going to need a little help - and that's what you'll get in this book.

The really cool part about all of this is that it's so easy - just believe in yourself and take the steps outlined in this book. Stop doubting yourself and watch your thoughts. When you notice negative thoughts, just say to yourself, "I'm now canceling this negative thought and replacing it with this more positive affirmation of my true desires."

A Little Experiment

In fact, you don't even need to be that formal about it - but reciting something to that effect in your head is a great way to distract yourself from the negativity you're dealing with, and then it's important that you actually follow through and replace the thought with a positive one.

For example, let's say you are calling a creditor who you know to be a narcissistic jerk to explain why your payment will be late. Before you call, you might worry and tell yourself that they won't understand, and that they'll be rude or nasty to you.

When you make that call, you find that your fears come true. And here's the interesting part…it came true because you believed it would.

Next time a situation like that presents itself, visualize yourself being clearly understood and empathized with by your creditor. Visualize the situation working out to your best advantage, and really know it. Tell yourself things will work out in your favor, and really believe it.

I'll bet you have a different outcome this time. Give it a shot. You won't regret it!

Bottom line: If you can believe it, you can achieve it. It's a fact.

Start on the Road to Emotional Abuse Recovery

If you're dealing with a toxic family member or friend, you've probably got a lot of someone else's thoughts floating around in your head. You might think you're not good enough. You might think that your feelings and thoughts aren't genuine or relevant to the world, and you might even feel like a big fake when you do try to follow your dreams, simply because you've heard for so long that you're not worthy, whether directly or indirectly.

If you're struggling with a toxic relationship, especially a family-based one, you may have had so much conditioning that you aren't even sure which way is up.

The first step to healing is to start within your own head. You have to change those thoughts and limiting beliefs that are holding you back. Once you fix yourself, you can make the choices you need to make to remedy the situation.

Let's start here.

When I was in my own toxic family situation, I struggled with feelings of hopelessness, worthlessness and more. I felt like nothing I did or said was genuine or worth knowing about, like I had to hide who I was in order to conform to the expectations of my toxic family member.

But I learned some important lessons as I began the healing process, and I want to share them with you. If you're currently in this situation, you may have never heard these things - and when you first read them, you probably won't even believe them. But these are truths - and you keep reading them until you get it.

Changing your mind will help you to change your life. I'm living proof it works.

The 10 Most Important Things You Need to Know if You're in a Toxic Relationship with a Narcissist

As someone who has survived and thrived despite previously experiencing narcissistic abuse in my life, I have a few really important things to tell you if you're currently dealing with it - and I want you to read this brief list five times. And then once each day until it gets into your head - these things are so important to understand if you're ever going to recover from the emotional abuse you're suffering.

1. You are a real person with legitimate concerns, thoughts, feelings and aspirations.
2. You are good enough.
3. You don't need anyone's approval or endorsement to help you succeed. You can get validation through success in your own, self-dictated endeavors.

4. It isn't about you and that it isn't your fault. You aren't bad or broken.

5. You can literally do almost anything you want to do if you simply decide to do so. If you choose to do it, you'll be compelled to take inspired action and you will make it happen.

6. You have something real to offer the world. You matter. You have value.

7. You can be exactly what you choose to be and choosing your own identity does not make you selfish, lazy, entitled or otherwise unsavory.

8. You get to choose my own identity every day. You decide who you are and how far you go.

9. You can compromise for someone you love to a certain point when it's time to choose your priorities and choose a path. But compromise means that both parties bend and both parties are satisfied with the outcome. It's not compromising to give up what you truly want in order to make someone else happy or to keep them from getting angry at you.

10. If you were to walk away from the toxic relationship, the world would not end. But it will be very difficult, and you'll have a lot of soul-searching to do. You might be surprised to find out how much the toxic person can affect who you are and what you believe. Personally, I had to reexamine everything I understood to be true.

Mean People Suck: 3 Top Life Hacks for Dealing with Your Everyday, Average Narcissists

Our ultimate freedom is the right and power to decide how anybody or anything outside ourselves will affect us. ~Stephen Covey

So, you're minding your own business and having a bright, bright sunshiny day. Everything seems to be going your way - your kids are getting along, the guy at Starbucks finally gets your order right and the lights are all green.

Then, it happens.

Some yahoo comes along and takes a crap in your Cheerios. Suddenly, your sunny outlook is replaced by the storm clouds of negativity. You start remembering all those little things that bother you, the stresses, the annoyances, and the general malaise sets in. The kids start fighting, the coffee gets cold before you can drink it and the lights turn red. You're irritated and ready to scream.

"Mean people really do suck. There you are, minding your own business, having a great day, and some snarky cashier, office person, or even a bus driver shreds your happy little bubble of a life into a million pieces," says Anne Lloyd in the Mean People That Suck blog. "All you can remember is that one jerk who ruined your day."

Lloyd is totally on-point. Dealing with negative people in your life totally sucks.

Most everyone has experienced this whole mean people phenomenon at one time or another, and when the negativity is doled out by a random someone in the world, it's easy to learn to change your mind and change your perspective - after all, you don't need to deal with these people on a consistent basis. Why should you let them steal your sunshine?

But sometimes, it's not some random bus driver or grocery store clerk who causes the icky feelings - it's someone you love - a stressed out spouse, a controlling parent, or a fair-weather friend, for example. Then it becomes a whole different thing - because you can't just walk away and never see or talk to that person again. He or she is a part of your life, probably a pretty important part.

So, what do you do? Are you doomed to walking around with a proverbial rain cloud over your head? What's the trick to dealing with negative people in your life - especially when you love them - all while keeping the sun shining in your world?

3 Best Practices for Dealing with Toxic People in Your Life

As a survivor of narcissistic abuse, a perception change is most likely in order, and you have to start with simply understanding exactly what and who you are dealing with here. Once you are able to recognize that toxic people in your life are seriously LIMITED in their abilities to function like normal human beings, it can truly empower you.

You round all of this out with self-love and unconditional self-acceptance, and you respect your boundaries.

Understand What's Happening

As children, we crave the approval of the people we love. We want our parents to be proud of us, we want our teachers to think we're smart and we want our friends to think we're cool. As we grow older, we often tend to accept what our loved ones think as fact, and we internalize their thoughts and judgments against us. We begin to think that maybe they're right, that we're not good enough or that we really aren't as cool or smart as we thought.

But here's the thing that we forget. Our loved ones are human, just like we are, and in some cases, they're just plain wrong.

"Just because someone is concerned for your welfare does not mean that their advice or input has value," says writer Peter Murphy. "For example, I know a lot about peak performance. I do not know much about car maintenance. If I ever offer you advice on rebuilding a car engine run as fast as you can! My input would have little or no value."

Same deal with your loved ones - sometimes they may be negative about you or your choices because they can't understand or simply don't know how to think positively about the situation. And their lack of understanding can lead to unreasonable anxiety about your life - which, of course, makes them feel justified in throwing down some negativity on your (otherwise happy) ass. You have to learn to distinguish between valuable advice and unreasonable negativity.

Approve of Yourself

By nature, we seek the approval of the people we love. And for those of us who have dealt with toxic people, approval-seeking can become very dangerous for us – we are almost addicted to the idea of people liking us; often so much so that we are willing to give up our own comfort and to go without things we need in order to make someone else happy.

At the very least, in many cases, we can feel limited and stifled by the constraints that maintaining such approval can impose on us. Some people in our lives offer conditional love, which means that they can't (or won't) treat you with love or respect unless you can be the person they want you to be.

When we don't fit into the neat little boxes that our loved ones (and our society) have set out for us, we are often ostracized or shunned, sometimes by those closest to us. And, if we require the approval of those we love to be happy, we set ourselves up for conditional self-acceptance - so when we're doing what "they" think we should, we think we're allowed to feel good about ourselves (even if that nagging feeling in the pit of our stomachs is telling us that we're not on the right path.) We become the victims of the limiting beliefs of the people around us.

We must learn to let go of the need to please the people we love, and start focusing on what's right for ourselves. We must claim our independence from negativity and judgment, following our hearts to find true peace. Be yourself, and proudly claim your place in this world.

When you are happy and at peace with yourself, you'll attract more happiness and peace into your world.

Change Your Mind, Change Your Life

I've said it till I'm blue in the face: you get back what you put out into the world. So, when you focus on the negativity in your life, the bad stuff, you'll attract more of it to yourself. When you maintain a mostly positive attitude, you draw more of the same into your life.

We must own our confidence and trust in ourselves and our intuition. Keep your eye on the prize, and always expect the best - because the fact is, you get what you expect. Learn to let go of the past and focus on the positive things you've got coming toward you today.

If you've been hurt by someone you love, you must forgive that person in order to heal and move forward in peace. At all costs, try to avoid internalizing the negativity of others, and focus instead on the wonderful things in your life.

Bottom Line

We can't control the people around us, no matter how hard we try. Practice accepting yourself and the people you love for who they are and stay focused on what really matters. Be true to yourself and stay on the path that you know is right for you. Understand negativity for what it and find the approval you seek within yourself, for when you manage to achieve this new level of understanding, the rest will fall into place.

Narcissists in Relationships: Where Gaslighting Begins

"Understanding how a narcissist works is the key to living or working with one. If you can understand his or her behavior, you may be able to accept it as you realize their behavior is NOT a result of anything you did or said despite them emphatically blaming you. If you can accept their behavior and not take the abuse and other actions personally, you can then emotionally distance yourself from the narcissist. If you can emotionally distance yourself, you can either cope with the narcissist or garner the strength to leave." ~ Alexander Burgemeester, The Narcissistic Life

You might be surprised to learn a few of these facts about gaslighting.

1. The beginning of a relationship with a narcissist can be very deceptive; in most cases, a narcissistic relationship begins just like any other - with the

standard phases of initial attraction, infatuation and eventually falling in love.
2. There is no single "type" that a narcissist typically goes for, technically - there are no parallels to be drawn among the partners of narcissists as far as height, weight, eye color, race or any other physical or cultural characteristic.
3. While there seems to be no "ideal" or "standard" mate/friend/spouse for a narcissist, there are certain similarities about the relationships. For example, the narcissist typically begins a new relationship with a "honeymoon" period, during which everything seems perfect, almost too good to be true.
4. Living in a relationship with a narcissist can be anything from exciting and exhilarating to soul-sucking and traumatic. And it usually is one or the other - depending on what day it happens to be. You might compare it to a type of emotional rollercoaster.
5. And a narcissist cannot exist without someone to adore, submit to their will, be available at their whim and the "someone" must be willing to disparage themselves to the narcissist's benefit. The narcissist's whole identity really

> depends on it - it's called narcissistic supply.

So, what draws a person into this type of relationship and keeps them there? Keep reading, and I'll fill you in.

3 Shocking Common Qualities Among the Partners of Narcissists

"The inherently dysfunctional 'codependency dance' requires two opposite but distinctly balanced partners: the pleaser/fixer (codependent) and the taker/controller (narcissist/addict," says Ross Rosenberg. "Codependents - who are giving, sacrificing, and consumed with the needs and desires of others - do not know how to emotionally disconnect or avoid romantic relationships with individuals who are narcissistic - individuals who are selfish, self-centered, controlling, and harmful to them. Codependents habitually find themselves on a "dance floor" attracted to partners who are a perfect counter-match to their uniquely passive, submissive and acquiescent dance style."

While physically, culturally and otherwise, the victims of narcissism aren't the same, there are certain qualities that typically unite them. I'm going to use the "she" pronoun here but note that there is no single sex that is a typical victim (although, to be fair, men reportedly make up the majority of narcissists).

First, she must be insecure or at least have a distorted sense of reality, if you expect her to stick around. Otherwise, she'll be out on the first or second exhibit of narcissism, early on in the relationship.

She will likely often belittle and demean himself, while glorifying the narcissist and putting him on an untouchable pedestal.

As a result, the partner becomes the victim, which works fine for her - she has a tendency to punish herself. Maybe she's even a bit of a masochist. She probably feels like she "deserves" this life of torment.

She's his eternal scapegoat, always put-upon and putting her own needs last.

"It is through self-denial that the partner survives," says Sam Vaknin, author of Malignant Self-Love. "She denies her wishes, hopes, dreams, aspirations, sexual, psychological and material needs, choices, preferences, values, and much else besides. She perceives her needs as threatening because they might engender the wrath of the narcissist's God-like supreme figure."

Victims of narcissism often call themselves "people-pleasers" or "diplomats," but the truth is, they are often so downtrodden in relationships that they just become changed, reactive versions of their former selves.

"When you are the partner of a narcissist, you are there to project the image he wants for you - that he wants his partner to project," writes Diane England, PhD. "Of course, your house and lifestyle probably fall into this category, too. They are all about making statements to others he wishes to impress, not about providing you with the type of environment you might find comfortable or restful - an environment that feeds your soul."

The 3 Stages of Gaslighting

If you're involved in a toxic relationship with a narcissist (or even a person with NPD or narcissistic personality disorder), then you have probably been the victim of gaslighting at some point.

The term "gaslighting" comes from a 1944 movie called Gaslight in which a husband tries to slowly drive his wife insane to cover up a big secret. There are three primary stages of gaslighting, as it applies to the psychological term.

Gaslighting Stage One: Disbelief

"The process of gaslighting happens in stages - although the stages are not always linear and do overlap at times, they reflect very different emotional and psychological states of mind," writes psychoanalyst Robin Stern in Psychology Today. "The first stage is disbelief: when the first sign of gaslighting occurs. You think of the gaslighting interaction as a strange behavior or an anomalous moment. During this first stage, things happen between you and your partner - or your boss, friend, family member - that seem odd to you."

So, in layman's terms - that means you'll find yourself wondering what just happened. You'll think the person just "sort of snapped" and that the behavior might be out of character. You'll be shocked at some of the things the narcissist says to you - and you'll find yourself going "huh?" when he reacts or responds to you. A gaslighter almost seems to go out of his way to make you wonder - but he's not really trying to do that.

He's just being himself - a narcissist.

Gaslighting Stage Two: Defense

"In the second stage, defense, the gaslightee has begun to second-guess himself," writes TheWeek.com's Shannon Firth.

This means that you start to wonder if maybe the narcissist is right - maybe you are the one to blame. You find yourself being constantly criticized by the narcissist and you being to think that you are really as slow, stupid, bad, lazy or whatever other rudeness is being spewed your way.

Again, often the narcissist doesn't even see what he's doing here - but you won't miss it. You'll feel almost exhausted by the constant barrage of insults and digs being thrown your way, and you might even vow to make personal changes in order to become whatever it is the narcissist says you're not. You lose a bit of yourself, really.

Gaslighting Stage Three: Depression

"By the time you get to this stage you are experiencing a noticeable lack of joy, and you hardly recognize yourself any more. Some of your behavior feels truly alien," according to Marriage Advocates. "You feel more cut off from friends – in fact, you don't talk to people about your relationship very much – none of them like your guy. People may express concern about how you are and how you are feeling – they treat you like you really do have a problem."

At this point, you're probably in need of a serious life overhaul. Whether you get professional help or you simply take your power back by recognizing the serious nature of the situation and taking appropriate action to make it change - you've got to do something.

Staying in a gaslighting situation is clearly dangerous for you as a person, but in some cases, it can become even more serious since some narcissists will abuse their victims physically too.

How can you tell if you're being gaslighted?

"Narcissism falls along the axis of what psychologists call personality disorders, one of a group that includes antisocial, dependent, histrionic, avoidant and borderline personalities. But by most measures, narcissism is one of the worst, if only because the narcissists themselves are so clueless." ~Jeffrey Kluger

If you've ever had a friend, family member or co-worker who is a narcissist or who suffers from narcissistic personality disorder (NPD), chances are you have been the victim of gaslighting, which is a manipulation technique they often employ to get what they want.

"Those who engage in gaslighting create a reaction - whether it's anger, frustration, sadness - in the person they are dealing with," writes Yashar Ali in a Huffington Post article. "Then, when that person reacts, the gaslighter makes them feel uncomfortable and insecure by behaving as if their feelings aren't rational or normal."

While the signs you're being gaslighted may seem "obvious" to some people, the fact is that when you're being manipulated by a narcissist, you can't always see the proverbial forest for the trees.

So if you find yourself feeling like you might be a little crazy (part of the whole gaslighting technique) - or even if you're aware that it's happening and want to recognize it as it happens - understanding the signs can be the first step to making your life a little better.

When you're aware of the behaviors that cause your narcissist to engage in gaslighting, you can react differently and change the course of the outcome. So what are the signs you're being gaslighted?

Top 10 Warning Signs You're Being Gaslighted

I'm going to make this super simple and give you a list. These are all things that I personally experienced during gaslighting and from what my clients, readers and viewers tell me, they are things that you may be able to relate to as well.

1. **Your Fears Are Used Against You** - Many narcissists are very charming, at least when they want to be. Often, they will listen to every word you have to say and file away any vulnerabilities you reveal for later use. For example, if you told a narcissist you felt insecure about your weight, he might later make discreet pokes at it, or in a romantic relationship, make comments about others who are thinner than you are - in any case, the narcissist's goal is to make you doubt yourself so that you become more dependent on him.

2. **You Don't Know Your Own Mind** - Some narcissists will claim to know what you (or others) are thinking - and if you deny that your mind's working the way they believe it is, they might

just secretly think you're lying. They might make a face or a gesture to indicate it - or in the most extreme cases of NPD, they might actually tell you that you're lying - and even accuse you of lying to YOURSELF. Because of course, as narcissists, they can't be wrong.

3. **You Don't Know What's Normal** - If you are regularly being told that things are normal when, deep down, you know for sure they are not, you're likely the victim of gaslighting. For example, say your toxic boss asks you to blatantly lie to a client about the safety of an item. When you refuse, you might be told that ALL employees lie on behalf of their employers and that if you don't want to be a team player, maybe you should find another position.

4. **You're "Diagnosed" With Major Issues** - When a narcissist is lying or manipulating a friend, coworker or loved one, and isn't getting his way, he may turn up the intensity by questioning your sanity. You might be called paranoid, stressed out - too sensitive or even hormonal. He might even tell you that you need therapy or

meds to get through it. Again, it's all about being in control.

5. **You Doubt Your Own Beliefs and Perceptions** - You're told that what you know to be true is not real. For example, if your narcissist mother tells you that your significant other is a loser and that you need to dump them, after a while, you could start to believe it and might even end up sabotaging the relationship because you begin to question your own judgment, thanks to regular conditioning during visits, phone calls and emails with her.

6. **You Can't Remember Anything Anymore** - The narcissist is infamous for selective memory; that is, they will deny that he said something that upset you if you confront them on it, or they will promise to do something and later tell you that it never happened. They might also use creative language to downplay his behavior and act as though your reaction is totally out of line.

7. **You Lie to Keep the Peace** - You aren't a liar by nature and you don't lie to other people in your life. But due to the

extreme stress caused by upsetting or angering the narcissist, you might find yourself at least bending the truth a little in order to avoid the verbal/physical abuse that is sure to follow any discussion or situation that is against the narcissist's "rules."

8. **You Stop Trying to Be Heard** - As humans, we are programmed to share our experiences and thoughts with the people in our lives. But when you're dealing with a narcissist and there are signs you're being gaslighted, you eventually might just give up. You stop talking about yourself around the narcissist and depending on the depth of your relationship with him or her; you might even stop talking about yourself altogether. Then one day, when someone asks you a question about yourself, you're stumped. You might even forget HOW to talk about you.

9. **You Start Thinking Maybe You Really Are the Crazy One** - The intensity of a narcissist's manipulation tactics can really get to a person. And when you are looking for a solution (AKA a way to just END the disagreement or argument), you might just convince yourself that

the narcissist is right - that there are things you could be doing better. And maybe you start to think that maybe his behavior WAS a logical reaction to your mistakes. Maybe you are the one who owes HIM an apology. And when you apologize, he eventually (probably) accepts your apology, only to later throw your "bad behavior" back in your face when it serves him.

10. **You Are Depressed** - As a narcissist wears down his victim, she may become depressed and anxious. She will constantly question herself and feel generally hopeless. If you're in this situation, you might feel exhausted from the roller-coaster ride your narcissist has been taking you on - and you might even think you're just a little oversensitive (thanks to the NPD manipulation tactics you're being subjected to.) You get confused and start to feel disoriented. And thanks to all those references to your paranoia and memory issues, you're likely to seek help for depression rather than the actual problem - the gaslighting narcissist in your life.

Even the so-called normal relationships in our lives can suffer from misunderstandings and miscommunications, but when someone starts using the manipulation tactics involved in gaslighting, chances are they might also be a narcissist - and if you're going to maintain a sense of self, you've got to start making some changes in your life.

Do you recognize any of the signs you're being gaslighted as part of your reality?

Narcissistic Rage and Narcissistic Injury: 6 Ways to Diffuse a Raging Narcissist

"Half the harm that is done in this world is due to people who want to feel important. They don't mean to do harm, but the harm [that they cause] does not interest them. Or they do not see it, or they justify it because they are absorbed in the endless struggle to think well of themselves." ~ T. S. Eliot

Narcissistic rage and narcissistic injury go hand in hand. While they often claim that their raging behavior is related to stress, the opposite is true. In fact, a narcissistic rage is triggered usually by some perceived insult, criticism or disagreement that results in a narcissistic injury.

The average raging narcissist thinks that her victim intentionally caused this so-called "injury" and that the victim did so with a hostile motive.

The reaction to this trigger is often intensely disproportionate to the actual "offense" committed by the victim - and invariably, the victim in these situations sees the narcissist as unreasonable, out-of-control, mean or even just plain old crazy.

If you're the regular target of narcissistic rage, you need to know that it is REALLY not your fault! The rage isn't about you, and it never was - it's always been about the narcissist.

Surviving Narcissistic Rage and Narcissistic Injury: Diffusing a Raging Narcissist

When you find yourself the victim of this kind of rage, you have to respond logically, not emotionally.

"This is the catch-22," says Sam Vaknin, a self-proclaimed narcissist. "To try to communicate emotions to a narcissist is like discussing atheism with a religious fundamentalist. They employ a myriad of defense mechanisms to cope with their repressed emotions: projective identification, splitting, projection, intellectualization, rationalization."

Now, when I say respond logically, I don't mean that you should try to use logic or reason to help the narcissist calm down - this almost never works. In fact, during a narcissistic rage, there really isn't room for your opinion or side of the story at all - in fact, offering it will just prolong the confrontation.

Remember: it's not about you - it's about the narcissist. Try not to take it personally (even though the narcissist will stop at nothing to hurt your feelings and cause you to react - be prepared).

Diffuse a Raging Narcissist: Stay Calm and Avoid Reacting Emotionally

You've got to stay calm and if possible, simply remove yourself from the situation. If you can't do that, take a deep breath be prepared to bite your tongue. Don't bother to argue or try to reason with the narcissist. Instead, just let him know that you hear his concerns and avoid raising your voice or introducing any emotion into the conversation.

Diffuse a Raging Narcissist: Know the Patterns

First, understand that not a single thing you say will change the narcissist's feelings during the rage. It doesn't matter if she's arguing that the sky should be red instead of blue - she's right as far as she's concerned, and there's nothing that you or anyone else could say to change her mind. Remember: it's about controlling the situation and being perceived by you as perfect. Any evidence that she's losing control or not being perceived as perfect will further incite the rage. In order to end a rage, a narcissist needs to feel safe and in control of the situation - so if you simply want to end the temporary situation, then you may need to say whatever she needs to hear to feel that way again - especially if your safety is at stake, but even if it's just your emotional well-being you're trying to protect.

Understanding the Hidden Messages in Narcissistic Rage

The Narcissist in Public

An interesting thing about most narcissists - being the charming and outgoing people they are, they project a public image of being "fun" and "laid-back," but in private, it's a whole other story. Behind closed doors, a narcissist feels safe to release his rage. And since he's so often the life of the party, the nice guy and the charmer that everyone loves to hang out with (in public, anyway), many people won't have any idea what kind of person they're really dealing with. So, unless someone personally witnesses this narcissistic rage, they can't understand what life is like for the victim/target of the narcissistic rage - especially when it's a lover, parent or family member.

The Narcissist and Projection

As the victim of a narcissistic rage, you've likely been accused of being selfish or of ignoring the narcissist's emotional or physical needs, of being dishonest, arrogant, lazy or any number of other insulting descriptives. But what's really happening most of the time is projection - narcissists project their own inadequacies onto their victims. So as usual, it's all about the narcissist, not about you.

The Narcissist and Selective Memory

Narcissists are infamous for their selective memories. They may claim they said something that they never really did - and then get angry at you for "not listening." Or they might even deny saying something that you KNOW they did say, but now regret. And, they're likely to contradict themselves in the same breath, lashing out at anyone who points it out to them. In either case, you might feel like you're going a little crazy when this happens - and it's a sign of gaslighting.

The Narcissist and You

When you love a narcissist, you have to understand your role in her life. A narcissist really doesn't have any interest in being emotionally or intellectually stimulated by the people in her life. In fact, feedback of any kind can be perceived as a threat.

People who love narcissists have really clear roles in their lives: they are the primary source of "narcissistic supply;" that is, they are expected to supply the narcissist with the admiration, respect, love and attention the narcissists believe they deserve. But when these "suppliers" fail in their mission (in the narcissist's opinion), the rage often turns against them.

"A passive witness to the narcissist's past accomplishments, a dispenser of accumulated Narcissistic Supply, a punching bag for his rages, a co-dependent, a possession (though not prized but taken for granted) and nothing much more," Vaknin writes. "This is the ungrateful, FULL TIME, draining job of being the narcissist's significant other."

Overcoming Your Narcissist: Top 10 Strategies to Overcome Anger and Gain Peace

So, here's the deal. When you're dealing with a narcissist in a gaslighting situation, you're bound to get pretty upset at times - and when you allow him or her to affect you that way, you're just letting them win.

It's totally normal to get upset when someone employs gaslighting manipulation strategies on you.

In fact, feelings of anger are normal and even appropriate at times. However, it's important to deal with anger effectively. Uncontrolled anger can create additional burdens on your relationships and in your life.

If your anger is getting the best of you, investigate a few alternatives to help keep it under control.

Try these techniques to deal with anger in the most positive way you can.

Begin to deal with anger when you first notice it. It's much easier to control any emotion at the onset. As you become more stimulated, it's more challenging to think clearly and rationally. Notice when you're starting to become upset and you can stop anger in its tracks.

Count to 10 and breathe. Giving yourself a moment to gather your thoughts can help to defuse the situation. Take the time you need. There's nothing wrong with taking a short timeout.

Avoid saying anything while in an angry state. Speaking while in a negative mental state can create further challenges. Remember all the times you wish you'd kept quiet instead of lashing out. Think before speaking and you'll save yourself a lot of apologizing later.

Focus on solutions. Whatever we focus on tends to expand. Directing your focus to finding an answer to the issue increases the odds of a positive resolution.

Distract yourself. The might be seen as avoiding the situation but focusing on something else for a while can overcome anger enough to permit seeing things more clearly. Choose to think about something that makes you happy.

When your emotions are settled, you can return to the situation with a renewed ability to gain peace.

Put a smile on your face. Emotions follow action. Smiling is your choice. If you smile, you'll feel better and be in a more useful mental state for finding a solution.

Seek to understand those who have angered you. If you understand the reasons the other person angered you in the first place, you might find it was just a simple misunderstanding. It's also possible you made a mistake and can then rectify it.

Be certain you have a valid reason for your anger. You might find there's no reason to be angry at all.

- Apply logic to the situation. Consider the likely outcome of being angry. Is it really going to help you? Is the situation likely to improve or get even worse? Seeing the negative outcome of continuing with your anger might be enough to put a stop to it.

- Make peace the priority. As the saying goes, "You can be right, or you can be happy." A feeling of equanimity trumps anger every time. Value your peace of mind more than you value your ego or holding on to negative feelings.

- Consider the impact on your relationship. When we say or do things in anger, it's not always possible to take them back because the damage has already been done. Your relationship is more important to you than the issue causing the anger.

With your spouse, child, significant other, close friend, or other loved one, keep the fact that you love them at the forefront of your mind, even in a disagreement. It will help you think more clearly about the issue.

It's important to maintain positive relationships with your boss and coworkers. Consider the consequences that your anger could have on your job.

Anger is a normal emotion, yet has the power to be very destructive. There are many ways to deal with anger effectively and peacefully. Focus on understanding and finding solutions to upsetting situations.

Top 10 Tips for Enhancing Your Emotional and Mental Health

Your current lifestyle may not be conducive to maintaining your emotional and mental health. Our society is overworked, overstressed, and too focused on things that don't support good psychological well-being.

Being proactive and doing things that foster good mental health can be a powerful way to enrich the quality of your day-to-day life.

Apply these tips on a daily basis:

1. No man is an island. Having positive and healthy relationships with others plays an important part in psychological health.

2. Keep your body healthy. Poor physical health can result in difficulties with mental health. The better you feel physically, the better you'll feel psychologically, too.

3. Regularly challenge yourself. While having too much stress in your life is negative, having

too little can be just as bad. We all need a certain amount of stress to thrive and stay sharp. If your life lacks any challenge, create some.

* Develop a goal and strive to meet it. There will most definitely be some stress and challenges along the way.

4. Learn how to deal with stress effectively. Most of us have self-soothing habits that fail to address the cause of stress. Some of us deal with stress in ways that make the situation worse. If you're financially stressed, eating a tub of ice cream will still leave you broke, but you'll also end up gaining weight. Seek positive solutions instead.

* Activities such as exercising, spending time with a friend, or reading a book can be healthy options for lowering your stress.

5. Spend time each day on an enjoyable activity. It might be playing the piano or taking your dog for a walk. It doesn't matter, as long as you concentrate on things other than work and necessary routines.

6. Practice the art of forgiveness. Anger and grudges accomplish little. They put you in a

vicious mental cycle that degrades your sense of well-being. Every second you're angry or upset is a second you're unhappy.

7. Give your time to others. Helping someone in need is a great way to boost the way you feel about yourself. It's also a great way to meet others that are also caring and giving.

* Consider a group of people you'd like to help and find an organization that services them.

8. Learn how to quiet your mind. You mind rarely gets a rest, not even while you're sleeping. All night long you're likely tossing, turning, and dreaming. There are many ways to rest your mind: praying, meditating, and practicing mindfulness are just a few.

* Brains are restless. They're constantly thinking, predicting, and remembering. Learn how to control yours.

9. Ask for help. If you break your arm, you seek medical assistance. If you're having a psychological issue, there's no reason not to do the same. No matter what your challenge may be, there's someone available with the expertise to help.

10. Keep a journal. Recording your thoughts on paper after a long, hard day is therapeutic. It releases tension, provides a means of catharsis, and can give you a different perspective.

Emotional and mental health are both critical to your overall well-being. When any component of your health is suffering, it becomes much more challenging to be an effective parent, spouse, friend, or employee. All aspects of your life, especially your physical health, can suffer. Use these tips to address your psychological health. If you're not feeling better, it's time to seek help.

Staying in Control: Crucial Tactics for Managing Panic Attacks

Panic attacks are common for the victims of narcissists and their gaslighting manipulation techniques, but the intensity of the symptoms makes them unnerving. It's good to know that proper treatment can reduce or even eliminate the discomfort. Take a look at the facts about panic attacks and learn how to manage them.

4 Must-Know Facts about Panic Attacks

1. Understand the symptoms. Panic attacks affect your mind and body. You're likely to feel afraid and out of control. At the same time, your heart starts to race and you have difficulty breathing. You shake and sweat. Nausea, chills, and hot flashes are also typical.

2. Examine the causes. Researchers are still studying the exact causes, but there are some theories. Your family history or substance abuse can make you more prone to having panic attacks. You may have personal triggers that

lead up to an attack. On the other hand, you may suddenly feel tension that is unrelated to any external event.

3. Let go of your assumptions. Clearing up two myths about panic attacks will make them much easier to handle. While you may think you're having a heart attack or other serious issues, panic attacks do not pose any significant threat to your body. Similarly, you are still capable of making rational decisions even though you feel stressed.

4. Know the recovery rates. There are very effective treatments available. You may be able to find all the help you need in a book or online course or you may want to consult a therapist. By some estimates, successful treatment rates are 90% or higher.

9 Best Ways to Manage Panic Attacks

1. Talk with your doctor. A visit with your personal physician is a good place to start. They can test you to rule out any physical causes and recommend a course of treatment.

2. Consider medication. While you're working

on changing your habits, medication could ease your stress. Your doctor may prescribe antidepressants and anti-anxiety drugs.

3. See a therapist. Various forms of therapy can help. In particular, cognitive behavior therapy trains you to develop new ways of thinking and acting. You'll learn to spot your stress triggers and respond more constructively.

4. Breathe deeply. Skillful breathing soothes any kinds of stress. Practice drawing full breaths starting down in your abdomen and rising up into your chest and head. Try to spend as much time exhaling as you do inhaling.

5. Expose yourself to discomfort. Ironically, when we try to avoid difficult situations, we often make things worse because we miss the opportunity to witness our strengths and learn valuable lessons. Turn the cycle around starting with small steps.

6. Wait 10 minutes. Panic attacks feel eternal, but they actually last for only about 10 minutes. Reassure yourself that it will be over soon.

7. Watch what you eat. Your diet contributes to your wellbeing. Nutritious whole foods that stabilize your blood sugar make you feel calmer.

By contrast, alcohol and caffeine could aggravate your anxiety.

8. Exercise regularly. Physical activity is one of the best remedies for dealing with panic attacks. Sign up for a yoga class or take a morning run in your local park.

9. Seek support. Friends and family may have trouble understanding your needs if they are unfamiliar with panic attacks. Look for a support group or think about forming your own. Helping others may speed up your own healing.

Talk with your doctor about what treatment options are appropriate for your individual needs. Overcoming panic attacks will restore your peace of mind and help you to resume the activities that you love.

Self-Confidence Booster: 8 Step Action Plan for Recovering from Narcissistic Manipulation and Abuse

Reading self-improvement articles and books can be a good investment in yourself. However, unless you make a real effort to apply the strategies to your life, little is likely to change. There's a big difference between knowing how to do a pushup and doing 100 pushups each day. Knowing what it takes to become self-confident won't get the job done. Application is critical.

Follow this plan to take control of your self-confidence:

1. Embrace change. Change is uncomfortable, and there's a good reason for this. Scientists believe that humans are slow to change because whatever we're currently doing is perceived as successful. But our ancient brains had a different idea of what constituted success. In the distant past, staying alive was challenging, and any new behavior might lead to death.

Realize that the discomfort you feel when you try something new is simply old instinct rising to the surface. Being uncomfortable usually isn't a good reason not to do something. You can still move forward in spite of your discomfort.

Be happy that you're uncomfortable. It means you're doing something that might actually change your life. Continuing with your comfortable behaviors won't make anything different.

2. List the areas where your self-confidence is most lacking. Figure out where you're feeling a lack of confidence. It might be your ability to learn a new skill or a setting that requires public speaking. It might be in social situations. Once you target your weaker areas, you can start making the necessary adjustments.

3. Determine your beliefs surrounding the areas where you lack self-confidence. Sticking with the public speaking example, perhaps you're worried that you'll say something embarrassing or that your voice isn't pleasant. If you're uncomfortable in social settings, maybe you think that you're not interesting enough.

4. Find the fault with those beliefs. If you're uncomfortable in dating situations because of your weight, you could find examples of heavier people who have had a lot of success in romantic relationships.

Engage in self-exploration by asking yourself some probing questions. How did you develop this belief? Do you really know that it's true? Have you tested it?

5. Seek out a mentor. This doesn't necessarily mean you have to find a "guru" to hold your hand. But there are plenty of people who have confidence in the area where you're experiencing challenges. Ask for help from someone who's comfortable in an area where you lack confidence, such as in dating situations or public speaking.

It's much easier to be confident when you're an expert. Learn everything you can and you'll feel better about yourself.

6. Start small (but start). If you lack confidence in finding a potential romantic partner, try walking through the mall and making eye contact with those you find

attractive. Then progress to smiling and saying hello. The next step could be to stop them and ask for directions.
Being confident with one step makes the next one possible.

7. Track your progress. It's important to see the progress you're making. Without progress, you won't stick with your plan. Measure your anxiety on a subjective 1 to 100 scale in different situations. Celebrate when you see progress! Check out my app support at DailyCoach.app.

8. Evolve your plan over time. Just as the same workout routine leads to stagnation, working on your self-confidence in the same fashion over a long period of time will lead to less than optimal results. Constantly evaluate and tweak your action plan.

If you lack confidence in yourself, it's hard to try new things or grow as a person. Create an action plan that addresses your self-confidence levels and strive to achieve the level of confidence you deserve.

6 Tips for Overcoming Adversity

In many ways, life seems to be one trial after another. Of course, this is especially true for the victims of gaslighting. Of course, just like everyone, regardless of our emotions and stress levels, we've got to successfully navigate these trials. The exact hurdles will differ from person to person. We all have challenges, though, so don't feel alone.

What's important is not what you're facing but how you choose to see it and deal with it.

Some of us seem to have an uncanny ability to successfully deal with any obstacle, while others struggle. We can all learn to be part of the former group.

Try these tips to make overcoming adversity easier:

1. Practice acceptance. Many of us choose to practice avoidance, which only allows the challenge to grow in size and complexity. You're taking the first step toward victory if you can accept what's happening in your life. It's hard to find a solution if you refuse to acknowledge that there's an issue.

2. Consider the advantages of the situation.
It's not easy to find the bright side of challenging times. But, focusing on the negative only makes the situation more difficult. Your efforts at positive thinking might feel a bit contrived at first, but the habit will feel more natural in time. Simply ask yourself, "What is the advantage of this situation?"

3. Use all of your available resources.
Consider all the resources you have available to you.

Friends and family: You may feel like isolating yourself when you're struggling but spending time with those that care about you can make the tough times much easier. If you're lacking a good support system, now is the time to strengthen existing ties and forge new ones.

Ask for help: Many people feel as if it's rude to just offer their assistance. They're waiting for you to ask! So ask and get the help you need. It's surprising how many people are willing to help, if you'll just make the request.

Utilize your inner resources: Be determined to find a solution. Practice having faith and confidence in yourself. If you believe everything will work out, it usually will. You largely get what you expect.

4. Focus on solutions. When you focus on something, it tends to magnify it in your mind, so avoid spotlighting the negative ramifications of your situation. Instead, focus on finding and executing a solution. Just take it step by step. You'll overcome your challenge before you know it.

The solution to your challenge can often involve unpleasant steps, such as ending a relationship or picking up a second job. The key is to visualize a positive outcome and simply do the work required. Just keep the outcome in mind.

5. Be persistent. Few challenges can withstand persistence. If you apply your best solution and things don't work out, adjust your approach and keep moving forward. It will probably take less effort and time than you think to turn things around. Persistence is paramount to any success.

6. Consider those who have been successful and faced greater adversity. The world is full of

examples of folks who have overcome amazing odds.

For example, we all know the story of Helen Keller, who became both blind and deaf at a very young age. Despite her extreme challenges, she became a highly educated and influential woman at a time when very few women were able to pursue higher education. And we all remember her because she changed the way people in her condition could experience the world.

We all face the challenges of adversity on a regular basis, and for those of us who have experienced narcissistic abuse, this can feel debilitating. But you want to be happy, and you want to be successful. You DESERVE that.

And you know that the most successful people are able to deal with adversity with a minimal amount of self-generated mental drama. Simply stay focused on executing possible solutions and utilize all of your available resources. Even when your toxic relationship ends, you will still want to keep these "overcoming" skills sharp. They will come in handy nearly every day.

8 Ways to Harness the Power of Personal Boundaries

Personal boundaries are important for several reasons, and especially if you're dealing with a narcissist and gaslighting issues. They serve as barriers to protect your self-esteem. They are also tools for establishing limits with others and communicating that you won't tolerate certain behaviors. Those without personal boundaries commonly end up in less than ideal situations and relationships.

Without limits, you're a victim to the whims of those around you. Personal boundaries are about respecting yourself and demanding respect from others.

Establish healthy personal boundaries with these tips:

1. Value yourself. You have the ability to set your own boundaries as you see fit. Few people will treat you better than you demand, so take responsibility for taking care of yourself. Unfortunately, no one else is going to take responsibility for your well-being.

2. Define yourself. You get to decide how you do it. Not the narcissist in your life, and not anyone else. YOU decide who you are, what you want to be, and how you deserve to be treated. What are you willing to accept from others? What are you no longer willing to accept?
If you don't define yourself, the rest of the world will do it for you. And you won't like it.

3. Put yourself on your priority list. Others are important, but they're not any more important than you. This can be tough for empaths and caregivers to accept! If you take care of yourself first, you're in a better position to take care of others. Running yourself ragged for others really isn't helping anyone. You'll be a better parent, spouse, and employee if you take good care of yourself.

4. Consider where you need to set limits in your life. Maybe you need to put an end to volunteering to work Saturdays or stop accepting emotional abuse from your boyfriend. Maybe you're just too willing to loan money to people that never pay you back. You get in life what you're willing to tolerate. What are you no longer willing to tolerate?

5. Make your boundaries firm and clear. This

is a BIG one for survivors. The codependency issues we develop in toxic relationships make it difficult to set real boundaries. So be careful but be firm. In other words, make your boundaries reasonable, but clear to others. If others know where you stand on certain issues, there's less chance for confusion or miscommunication. It's possible to have boundaries that are too strict. But for us, it's better to be a bit strict than to be too lax. You can take your time as you recover and relax some boundaries if you feel safe doing so, but don't rush it.

6. Be flexible. You don't have to follow the rules 100% of the time. Decide who and what you want to let in and what's best to keep out. Studies have shown that people with some flexibility in their personal boundaries tend to have to best combination of happiness and success. Being too rigid can be just as problematic as being too lax. In other words, protect yourself, but don't stop living.

7. Learn to say no when needed. Boundaries are limits on what you'll accept from others. Avoid falling victim to the tendency to make everyone else happy. Healthy boundaries and being a little selfish go hand-in-hand. Try saying "no" to someone today. The world won't come end. I promise.

8. Communicate openly. When people cross your boundaries, it's up to you to inform them. Many times, this is as simple as refusing a request. You may be required to provide more explanation in other instances. And hey, remember that no one else can give you what you want if you don't provide feedback.

Having boundaries is an exercise in caring for and respecting yourself. You have the right to expect a certain level of respect and consideration from others.

If your lack of personal boundaries is creating challenges for you, now is the time to start taking better care of yourself. Adequate boundaries are not only good for your self-esteem and general mental health, but for all other aspects of your life. You also put yourself in a better position to care for your friends and family.

ions & Reflections for the Victims of Gaslighting and Other Forms of Narcissistic Abuse

For the next seven days, spend a few minutes each day reading and reflecting on the affirmations and reflection questions listed here. Write in your journal or on your favorite journaling app to answer the questions. Then, as the day progresses, think about your answers and how they can start helping you take back your life.

This will help you to start creating some serious personal change, in small baby-step format. Always the best way in my opinion.

Are you ready to start day one? Turn to the next page and let's do this.

Day 1: You Are Blessed.

Today, remember first that you are blessed. Focus on those things which you want and not those things that make you feel unhappy; remember - you bring about what you think about, so focus on what you really do want more of in your life.

Today's Affirmations:

1. Blessings follow me wherever I go.

2. In all things, I am blessed, and I make it a point to take notice of all the good in my life. Even if I experience challenging events, I always remember how blessed I am.

3. I always have plenty of whatever I need. And often, I have more than enough. I am loved abundantly, and I have plentiful love to give in return.

4. Infinite resources are at my fingertips. In the realm of money, I always have enough to cover my basic needs and to meet many of my desires, too.

5. If I experience times when I feel a lack of abundance, I remind myself that, in truth, I have all that I require. Whether I am employed or unemployed, partnered or single, with lots of kids or no kids at all, I feel blessed in a multitude of ways.

6. Nothing I can do can destroy or wash away the many blessings that come my way. And to be fully satisfied with life, all I have to do is remember the abundance that is available to me.

7. My universe is plentiful and my heart is abundant. Blessings come to me freely, and I cultivate gratitude for it.

8. Today, I make time to contemplate the ways in which I am a blessed. I regularly experience gratitude for all of the wonderful things in my life. And I seek out opportunities to demonstrate this gratitude by living with a sense of abundance.

Self-Reflection Questions

Ask yourself the following questions and journal or blog the answers.

1. How have blessings manifested in my life in the past few weeks?

2. What are three things I can be thankful for today?

3. What are some positive surprises that have arisen from events I initially perceived as negative?

Day 2: I am the best version of myself.

Today, I want you to reflect on what it means to be the best version of YOURSELF. This doesn't mean becoming what anyone else expects you to be, but rather, it means becoming EXACTLY the person you truly know you've always meant to be. You get to decide. Remember that as you go about your day - you get to choose your own experiences.

Today's Affirmations:

Today, and every day, I am dedicated to self-development.

Each day, my life is filled with opportunity. I can choose to learn and grow in so many ways.

What motivates me most, however, are opportunities to live my highest vision of myself. Therefore, today and every day, I am dedicated to self-development.

My life is a path of endless growth. Because of this, I am forgiving of times when I may say or do something that I later wish I had done differently.

I seize every opportunity to make positive change in my life. Lucky for me, this includes each of my mistakes! So instead of seeing them as negative situations, I am thankful for them.

Each night before bed, I reflect on my day. In addition to assessing opportunities for change, I also give myself praise for the things I do well.

If I feel fatigued by the pressures of life, I remind myself of the many benefits I gain from my diligent pursuit of self-development. One of these benefits is inner peace instead of caving in under pressure. This contemplation always motivates me to renew my efforts, and I do so, invigorated.

Today, I am dedicated to self-development. I am thankful for every opportunity to re-create myself anew. And I recommit to growing toward my highest vision of myself, each and every day.

Self-Reflection Questions:

1. What are some of the self-development "projects" I have been working on lately?

2. Which projects challenge me most right now? Why? How can I overcome these challenges?

3. In what ways have I changed intentionally, for the better, over the past year or two?

Day 3: I love and approve of myself

What does it mean to love and approve of yourself? Well, it's not just thinking "hey, I don't suck." Nope. It's so much more than that. You've got to literally fall in love with yourself in the same way you fall in love with someone else. It sounds silly, but you've got to try it - how would you treat yourself if you were your own boyfriend (or girlfriend)? Think about that as you go about your day today!

Today's Affirmations:

1. I love and approve of myself, no matter what.

2. I am a valuable person and make worthwhile contributions to the world. Each day, in big and small ways, I remind myself of this. In any circumstance, I know that I am worthy.

3. Knowing my own value is important to me. Therefore, I cultivate thoughts that encourage me in what I am good at and forgive myself for any mistakes. I consciously invest my time and efforts in recognizing my own worth.

4. If I experience situations in which I begin to feel a lack of self-approval or self-love, I stop for a moment to take a deep breath. As I breathe, I remember that my value is independent of any external circumstances or actions I take. I love and approve of myself always.

5. My self-esteem radiates out from me and is reflected back by others. They easily see my sense and act in accordance with it.

6. If someone treats me in an unsatisfying way, I ask myself how I would prefer them to act. Then, I ensure that I am following my own good advice. I set the example for how I would like to be treated!

7. Today, I am thankful that I feel good about myself and treat myself with the utmost care and kindness. I seek out opportunities to exemplify self-love to enrich my life and the lives of those I love.

Self-Reflection Questions:

1. What are three things I can do to be kinder to myself today?

2. Are there times when I feel less than loving toward myself?

3. What can I do at those times to bolster my positive energy?

Day 4: My mind is clear and focused.

As the victim of someone who uses the gaslighting technique, it's common to experience what I like to call a "cluttered" mind. That means that your thoughts race and you can't always find the focus you need to get stuff done. So today as you go about your day, remember to keep your mind clear and focused on what you're doing in the moment. And as always, remember to think about what you do want and not what you don't!

Today's Affirmations:

1. I have an uncluttered mind.

2. I am free of all random thoughts and distractions. Whatever I choose as my focus becomes the sole direction of my mind. And I am thankful for the ability to direct my thoughts.

3. Each moment, I have choices about what I bring to pass in my life. I have heard that what we think, we create, and I believe that this is true. Much of my creative power lies in my ability to choose my thoughts. I set out in one direction and go only that way until I

decide otherwise. Nothing can distract me.

4. My focus is singular.

5. I am capable of excluding all else from my mind except for whatever I choose to focus on. If competing ideas arise, I consciously set them aside for another time. I engage in this on a thought-by-thought basis, cultivating awareness of my mind's contents so that I can choose its direction.

6. I am thankful for my focus, which allows me to be truly centered in who I am and what I want.

7. Since I can really be present in each moment, I can also fully enjoy the blessings that come my way. I can equally savor my partner's laughter, the warmth of sunshine, or the intensity of completing a long project. This is a gift, and I am thankful.

8. Today, I celebrate my mental clarity. My focus has contributed substantially to all of my accomplishments. Because of my uncluttered mind, I am easily able to manifest my highest vision of myself.

> And I intentionally cultivate my focus at every possible opportunity.

Self-Reflection Questions:

1. What topics are easiest for me to focus on?

2. Are there directions in which I would rather devote my mental energy?

3. What can I do today to continue to cultivate an uncluttered mind?

Day 5: I deserve the very best in my life

When you read today's title, what did you think? Do you believe you deserve the best things in life, or have you become so overwrought by the narcissistic abuse you're facing that you've forgotten how important you really are? Today I want you to consider this as you go around in the world: how would you treat yourself if you were taking care of a child? Do you think you'd beat yourself up for every small mistake? What if you were taking care of your own child? Or one you love? How would you treat him or her differently than you're treating yourself about now? Remember that you're just as good as everyone else and that you do deserve to have the very best in life. When you remember that and expect the very best, you'll get it.

Today's Affirmations:

I deserve to be pampered.

I consider myself worth every bit of luxurious treatment afforded to me! I know I am living in accordance with my life purpose, and that is enough to make me deserve all the pampering I can get.

I deserve to be pampered because I work hard.

I spend tireless hours getting the job done at the office and always ensure I put forth my best effort. I strive to achieve excellence and believe that I deserve relaxation and pampering for my fine efforts.

I take my chosen family and their well-being seriously. I pay attention to their needs to ensure they are met in the best way I know how. Sometimes, I sacrifice my desires, so they can be comfortable, but not for toxic people who would not return the favor. Only for those who truly love me. I am rewarded by their love because I am the person I (and they) need me to be.

I am treated like royalty by my family or the people I chose to be my family. They know that I love them unconditionally. I deserve the treatment they give me because my loving kindness and support to them is incomparable!

Today, I continue to live up to my firm belief that I deserve to be pampered. I work hard and love hard, and pampering is my just reward. I believe I am worth every positive treatment I receive.

Self-Reflection Questions:

1. Do I accept gifts graciously?

2. Do I recognize and acknowledge the efforts of others to express their gratitude to me?

3. Do I make time for myself, so I can be at my best for others?

Day 6: I am growing stronger in body, mind and soul.

Inner strength is the key to finding your true happiness regardless of the narcissist in your life. Today, I want you to remember that you are stronger than you ever thought you could be. Stand up on your two feet and take a stand today - remember that you are worth being treated with the same love and respect as everyone else - and don't accept anything less.

Today's Affirmations:

1. Each day, I grow stronger in mind, body, and soul.

2. Every day provides the possibility of growing stronger in every way. I seek out and take advantage of these opportunities. The possibility of growth is interesting and exciting to me.

3. I find ways to make my mind stronger. I constantly challenge my thinking and beliefs. Through challenge, I increase my capacity to overcome adversity.

4. I give my body the respect it deserves. I eat healthy food to provide my body with the nutrients it needs to be at its best. I exercise my body on a regular basis in order to be strong and fit. I get the sleep I need to feel alert and well rested each day.

5. I use prayer or meditation to nourish my soul. Giving these activities regular attention is a sure way to strengthen my spirituality.

6. Seeking small enhancements in each area of my life is easy and attainable. Small, incremental changes bring excellent results with a minimal amount of stress. I easily find opportunities to make these small changes.

7. Today, I am focused on strengthening every aspect of my being. I am embracing challenge as a chance for growth. My mind, body, and soul are growing stronger.

Self-Reflection Questions:

1. What can I do today to challenge my mind and increase its capacity to deal with adversity?
2. What changes can I make to my diet to strengthen my health?
3. How can I incorporate prayer or meditation into my life?

Day 7: I am grateful for all of the good things in my life.

I've said it before and I'll say it again - gratitude and love are the true keys to happiness. That's why a daily gratitude practice is so important! Today make a point of noticing and saying "thank you" for all of the beautiful and amazing good things in your life - even if you have to start with the simple fact that you woke up today and you're reading this book.

Today's Affirmations:

1. I give thanks daily for my focus in life.

2. I am confident in my ability to achieve my goals. Each day, I live with presence and conviction and, therefore, make good on my dreams. For this, I am intensely grateful.

3. I know that I can have what I want! All I need to do is focus. I put forth my intention and my dreams and desires are made manifest.

4. Focus is the biggest secret to my success. I pay close attention to what I want and then devote my energy to accomplishing my dreams.

5. Sometimes, achieving my goals requires greater effort than at other times. When this is the case, I am particularly thankful for my focus. Sustained effort requires motivation and motivation requires remembering why I am willing to put in some hard work. But when I focus on my goals, motivation comes easily.

6. If I feel distracted or scattered, I take a few moments to close my eyes and just breathe. I notice the sensations of my feet on the floor and my hands resting on my lap.

7. This simple exercise renews my focus by bringing me into the present moment. And when I am fully present, I feel gratitude for where I am and how far I have come.

8. Today, I make time to contemplate my many accomplishments. I am thankful for my focus in life, which enables me to have all that I want.

9. I seek out opportunities to cultivate this gratitude by paying attention to my deepest desires and pursuing them devotedly.

Self-Reflection Questions:

1. What are some of the things I have accomplished in the last year?

2. To what do I attribute these successes?

3. Are there aspects of my life that could benefit from greater focus?

About the Author

Angela Atkinson is a Certified Life Coach and the author of more than 20 books – many of which are currently available at Amazon.com.

A recognized expert on narcissism and narcissistic personality disorder who has studied and written extensively on narcissistic relationships, Atkinson has survived toxic relationships of her own.

Her mission is to help those who have experienced the emotional and mental devastation that comes with narcissistic abuse in these incredibly toxic relationships to (re)discover their true selves, stop the gaslighting and manipulation and move forward into their genuine desires – into a life that is exactly what they choose for themselves.

Along with her solution-focused life coaching experience, Atkinson's love of writing offers her the unique ability to share a new understanding of how life works for a whole new generation.

Atkinson's publishing resume is vast and varied and includes several years' experience in online journalism, including hard reporting as well as functioning as an editor in various iterations over the years.

In her life coaching practice, Atkinson's clients enjoy her personalized approach that allows and encourages them to become the best possible versions of themselves and to succeed in doing what they love most.

As you can see when you visit the freebies page at QueenBeeing.com, Atkinson's online daily magazine for women, she's all about paying it forward. She offers individual and group coaching for victims and survivors of narcissistic abuse at NarcissismSupportCoach.com.

Professional Affiliations

Atkinson is a member of the Society of Professional Journalists, including the St. Louis Pro Chapter and the national organization. She is also a member of the Universal Coach Institute alumni, the St. Louis Writers Guild, the

National Education Writers Association and the Freelancers Union. She studied journalism at Eastern Illinois University and earned her primary life coach certifications through the Universal Coach Institute.

One Last Thing

Thank you so much again for buying this book. If you haven't already, now would be an excellent time for you to run over and pick up your free gift. You can get it at QueenBeeing.com/FREEGIFT.

And, if you enjoyed this book and you have a moment, please add your review on the book's Amazon page. If you didn't enjoy the book, please reach out to me at angyatkinson@gmail.com and let me know what I can do better next time!

Other Books by Angie Atkinson

See the Most Current List at BooksAngieWrote.com.

On Narcissism and NPD
It's Not Supposed to Hurt: Overcoming Toxic Love and Narcissism in Relationships
Your Love is My Drug: How to Shut Down a Narcissist, Detoxify Your Relationships & Live the Awesome Life You Really Deserve, Starting Right Now
Navigating No Contact
Take Back Your Life: 103 Highly-Effective Strategies to Snuff Out a Narcissist's Gaslighting and Enjoy the Happy Life You Really Deserve (Detoxifying Your Life)

Gaslighting, Love Bombing and Flying Monkeys: The Ultimate Toxic Relationship Survival Guide for Victims and Survivors of Narcissistic Abuse

On Weight Loss and Self-Esteem

The Secret to Manifesting Your Perfect Body: Weight Loss From the Inside Out: How I Lost (and Kept Off) 100 Pounds Without Starving, Sweating or Hating ... (And How You Can Too)

227 Super-Simple, Super-Sexy Summer Slim-Down Strategies: The Smart Girl's Guide to a Very Sexy Summer (Project Blissful)

On Personal Success and Getting What You Want In Life

127 Powerfully Simple Life Hacks: Easy Ways to Empower Yourself and Improve Your Life in 30 Days or Less (Project Blissful)

69 INSTANT MANIFESTATION SECRETS: Quick and Easy Life Hacks for Remarkable Success (Project Blissful Book 4

Here Are The Keys to Explosive Personal Power: How to Stop Being a Doormat and Instantly Start Living the Life You Deserve (Project Blissful Book 3)

127 Powerfully Simple Ways to Be Really, Really Happy: Proven Happiness Hacks for Busy People (Project Blissful Book 8)

On Career Success

163 Simply Powerful Career Hacks Anyone Can Use: Get Where You Want to Go In Your Career, One Easy Step at a Time (Project Blissful Book 5)

The Practical Freelance Writer's Guide to Author Websites: How to Build, Manage and Promote a Freelance Writer Website (2010)

Contact Angie Atkinson

Get in touch with Angie via email at angyatkinson@gmail.com, on Twitter @angieatkinson or on Facebook at Facebook.com/coachangieatkinson.

Visit QueenBeeing.com/connect for more ways to get in touch.

Made in the USA
Monee, IL
27 June 2021